# Directions for Life
# Puzzle Book & Devotion

Victoria Roder

**Publishers Note:**

This is a work of fiction. All names, characters, places, and events are the work of the author's imagination. Any resemblance to real persons, places, or events is coincidental.

Cover Art: Val Muller

Copyright ©Victoria Roder 2013
All rights reserved
ISBN 13: 978-0615877204
ISBN 10: 0615877206

DWB PUBLISHING
www.dancingwithbearpublishing.com

To my brother, Arleigh, the Lord works in mysterious ways. If not for you, I would never have started creating puzzles. Follow the Lord and He will direct your path. God's blessings, "Ali BaBa".
Love, "Your Grubby Little Sister".

The Serenity Prayer by Reinhold Niebuhr
God Grant me the serenity to accept the things I cannot change;
Courage to change the things I can,
and the wisdom to know the difference.

To Alice Brandt thank you for solving puzzle after puzzle, and in some cases, the same puzzle several times!

## The Golden Rule

Life can throw different types of situations or struggles at us. Those situations can be as simple as stepping into a puddle and getting soaked, or as devastating as the death of a loved one. Annoyances and problems can help us develop our character. Our goal should be to have a heart that is Christ-like in all that we do.

Have you come across people that in a huff, abandon items in a store because they believe it is taking too long to check out? Have you observed a rude gesture because someone passed another vehicle on the road? We all experience frustration, impatience, devastation and anger. It is what we do with that anger and impatience that we are accountable for. If we keep the words of God written on our hearts, self control of our actions will follow.

As Christians we need to start with the basics. To live a life according to God's word, we must begin with love. Everyone you meet does not have to be your best friend, but out of love, even if you don't always agree with them, you can be kind. Jesus instructed, "'Love your neighbor as yourself.'" Matthew 22:39

Look up 1John 3:16 and record the verse.

" _____

_____

_____ "

Actions speak louder than words. How could you show God's love to a total stranger at the supermarket?

_____

_____.

Have you ever met anyone that disagrees or contradicts everything you say? If you ask three people how to build a birdhouse, you will probably receive three different answers. Keep in mind that different opinions aren't necessarily wrong—they are just a different perspective. There is more than one way to build a birdhouse.

In daily life, always fall back on the "Golden Rule". Look up Matthew 7:12 and record the "Golden Rule".

" _____

_____." "

As Christians, we need to keep in mind that we are not responsible for other people's actions, only our own actions, and reactions, to others.

What if waiting for what feels like an eternity, with patience, in line at the video store sets a positive example for another person? We may never know how our actions and reactions may affect or help other people, but that doesn't make them any less important in God's big picture.

Enjoy the puzzles and learn God's words and instructions for daily living.

**The Golden Rule Puzzles:**

Daily Frustrations
Good Verses Evil
Lean on Me
Bite Your Tongue

## Daily Frustrations

In the pairs of letters below, find the message from God on how to act with our daily frustrations.  Starting at **WD,** circle the first letter of the select pair. The second letter of the pair will tell you which direction to move.  L for left, R for right, U for up, and D for down.  Place circled letters in order on the lines below as you go.

| **WD** | FR | TU | NL | DR | UR | CD | AD | HU | JD |
|------|----|----|----|----|----|----|----|----|----|
| HR | AD | SL | FR | NU | PR | TR | YR | OD | AD |
| JU | TD | ER | CR | OU | KU | CD | NR | UD | TL |
| VD | EL | GL | SU | NL | JR | OD | SL | RR | SD |
| ER | RR | HD | TL | EU | HL | ID | SL | LD | EL |
| PR | ED | AR | PR | PU | TU | ND | EU | VL | YD |
| RU | LR | SD | OL | GL | EL | AR | MR | AD | BD |
| SR | ED | PL | HR | EU | HU | WR | OU | NR | ND |
| OD | LL | RR | TU | FL | OL | XD | WD | RL | EL |
| FD | RR | ID | SR | TL | YU | RD | OL | OR | SD |
| CR | HU | SR | **T** | IU | HU | TL | OU | LL | EL |

W __ __ __ __ __ __ __    __ __ __ __ __ __ __

__ __ __ __ __ __ __    __ __ __ __ __ __ __ __ __

__ __  __  __ __ __ __ __ __    __ __ __ __ __ __

__ __  __ __ __    __ __ __ __ __ __    __ __

__ __ __ __ __    T.     Philippians 1:27

## Good Verses Evil

|   | A | B | C | D | E |
|---|---|---|---|---|---|
| 1 | R | L | E | 9 | T |
| 2 | F | H | G | A | B |
| 3 | C | M | 1 | K | U |
| 4 | N | J | W | Q | S |
| 5 | Y | X | D | I | V |
| 6 | P | 7 | Z | 2 | O |

__  __  __  __   __  __  __  __   __  __
1B  6E  5E  1C   3B  3E  4E  1E   2E  1C

__  __  __  __  __  __  __
4E  5D  4A  3A  1C  1A  1C

__  __  __  __   __  __  __  __   __  __   __  __  __  __ ,
2B  2D  1E  1C   4C  2B  2D  1E   5D  4E   1C  5E  5D  1B

__  __  __  __  __   __  __   __  __  __  __   __  __
3A  1B  5D  4A  2C   1E  6E   4C  2B  2D  1E   5D  4E

__  __  __  __ .   __  __  __  __  __  __   __  __ : __
2C  6E  6E  5C     1A  6E  3B  2D  4A  4E   3C  6D    1D

**Lean on Me**

Skills Puzzle. Solve the math problem and match the letter to the number below.

2x8= __     5x4-3= __     40÷10= __     6+6= __     22÷2= __
  U              A                O              D            R

8x2÷8= __     30÷2-10= __     4003-4002= __     5+7-4= __
   H                I                  W                B

999-993= __     27÷3= __     2x5+3= __     64÷4-1= __
    F              S              E              N

15÷5= __     100÷10 __     46÷2-9= __     10÷2+2= __
  L              T                C                Y

__ __ __ __ __   __ __ __ __   __ __ __ __ __ __
14 17 11 11  7   13 17 14  2    4 10  2 13 11  9

__ __ __ __ __ __ __   __ __ __   __ __   __ __ __ __
8  16 11 12 13 15  9    17 15 12    5 15    10  2  5  9

__ __ __   __ __ __   __ __ __ __   __ __ __ __ __ __ __
1  17  7    7  4 16    1  5  3  3    6 16  3  6  5  3  3

__ __ __   __ __ __   __ __   __ __ __ __ __ __ __.
10  2 13    3 17  1    4  6    14  2 11  5  9 10

## Bite Your Tongue

| | | | | | |
|---|---|---|---|---|---|
| green | The | five | Lord's | violet | indigo |
| servant | three | must | not | red | quarrel |
| instead | orange | he | pink | gray | must |
| blue | be | kind | nine | to | everyone |
| able | tan | to | yellow | silver | teach |
| purple | not | mauve | seven | resentful | navy |

Direction#1: Circle all the number words and add the amounts together.  Place that number on the blank after the word Timothy, and then cross out the number words.

Direction #2: Cross out all the color words.

Direction #3: Place the remaining words in the order they appear from left to right on the blanks below to follow the Lord's direction.


___ ___ ___    ___ ___ ___ ___ ' ___    ___ ___ ___ ___ ___ ___ ___

___ ___ ___ ___    ___ ___ ___    ___ ___ ___ ___ ___ ___ ___,

___ ___ ___ ___ ___ ___ ___,    ___ ___    ___ ___ ___ ___    ___ ___

___ ___ ___ ___    ___ ___    ___ ___ ___ ___ ___ ___ ___,

___ ___ ___ ___    ___ ___    ___ ___ ___ ___ ___,    ___ ___ ___

___ ___ ___ ___ ___ ___ ___ ___ ___          2 Timothy 2:___

## The Truth Shall Set You Free

According to Webster's New World College Dictionary Fourth Edition, the definition of gossip is a person who chatters or repeats idle talk and rumors, especially about the private affairs of others.

My mother always repeated the phrase, "If you don't have anything good to say, don't say anything at all." The world would be a much quieter place if we all abided by this phrase. Keep your talk positive and encourage others with your words instead of tearing them down with gossip.

We are each accountable for our words toward each other and accountable for how we talk about others.

Can you think of a time you reacted to quickly and perhaps used harsh words toward another person?

_____

_____

Can you recall a time you used self-control and held your tongue?

_____

_____

**The Truth Shall Set You Free Puzzles:**

New in Christ
Truth
Hush
Self-Control

## New In Christ

ABCDEFGHIJKLMNOPQRSTUVWXYZ

On the lines below write the letter that comes between the top and bottom letter to finish the verse... *But now you must,*

Q H C   X N T Q R D K E   N E   Z K K
— — —   — — — — — — — —   — —   — — —
S J E   Z P V S T F M G   P G   B M M


R T B G   S G H M F R   Z R   S G D R D
— — — —   — — — — — —   — —   — — — — —:
T V D I   U I J O H T   B T   U I F T F


Z M F D Q   Q Z F D   L Z K H B D
— — — — —,   — — — —,   — — — — — —,
B O H F S   S B H F   N B M J D F


R K Z M C D Q   Z M C   E H K S G X
— — — — — — —   — — —   — — — — — —
T M B O E F S   B O E   G J M U L Z


K Z M F T Z F D   E Q N L   X N T Q
— — — — — — — —   — — — —   — — — —
M B O H V B H F   G S P N   Z P V S


K H O R
— — — —.
M J Q T

## Hush

Intersect the number and the bold letter to find the letter to place on the corresponding lines below, and solve the puzzle.

|   | A | B | C | D | E |
|---|---|---|---|---|---|
| **1** | R | L | E | 9 | T |
| **2** | F | H | G | A | B |
| **3** | C | M | Z | K | U |
| **4** | N | J | W | Q | S |
| **5** | Y | X | D | I | V |
| **6** | P | 4 | O | 2 | 5 |

5C 6C   4A 6C 1E   1B 1C 1E   2D 4A 5A

3E 4A 4C 2B 6C 1B 1C 4E 6C 3B 1C   1E 2D 1B 3D

3A 6C 3B 1C   6C 3E 1E   6C 2A   5A 6C 3E 1A

3B 6C 3E 1E 2B 4E   2E 3E 1E   6C 4A 1B 5A   4C 2B 2D 1E

5D 4E   2B 1C 1B 6A 2A 3E 1B   2A 6C 1A

2E 3E 5D 1B 5C 5D 4A 2C   6C 1E 2B 1C 1A 4E   3E 6A

2D 3A 3A 6C 1A 5C 5D 4A 2C   1E 6C

1E 2B 1C 5D 1A   4A 1C 1C 5C 4E.    Ephesians __: __ __

                                                6B  6D 1D

## Self Control

Directions: Starting at **QD,** circle the first letter of the select pair. The second letter of the pair will tell you which direction to move.  L for left, R for right, U for up, and D for down.  Place circled letters in order on the lines on the next page, as you go.

Start:                                         Everyone should be...

| **QD** | FR | KR | TR | OR | LD | WL | AD | HU |
|------|----|----|----|----|----|----|----|----|
| UR | IR | CU | RF | UV | ID | KR | GL | ND |
| JU | HR | AD | ML | WR | SR | TD | SL | SR |
| ED | PL | TD | WL | SD | NL | EL | RR | MU |
| AD | SU | OL | OU | LL | KL | AR | VR | ED |
| KR | AD | ND | GL | YR | PD | CR | OD | YR |
| OR | NR | DR | SD | TD | BR | EU | MR | ED |
| YU | AD | SL | LR | OD | OU | DD | SL | AD |
| EU | VL | NU | AL | WR | TU | OU | GD | NL |
| CD | CL | LD | BL | KB | CU | YD | RL | EL |
| ED | AU | YL | MU | DD | NL | AL | NR | TD |
| PR | TD | CD | UU | HL | PR | LR | AU | ED |
| EU | TR | HR | ED | FR | DU | EU | ID | DL |
| NU | YU | NL | WR | OR | RU | YD | NL | PL |
| TR | EU | IU | DL | EL | U | OL | AL | RL |

Q _ _ _ _  _ _  _ _ _ _ _ _,

_ _ _ _  _ _  _ _ _ _ _  _ _ _  _ _ _ _

_ _  _ _ _ _ _ _  _ _ _ _ _  _ _ _

_ _ _ _ _  _ _ _ _ _ _  _ _ _

_ _ _ _  _ _ _ _ _ _ _  _ _  _ _ _.

## Speak Truthfully

ABCDEFGHIJKLMNOPQRSTUVWXYZ

On the lines below write the letter that comes between the top and bottom letter to finish the verse. **Therefore each of you...**

L T R S    O T S    N E E

\_ \_ \_ \_    \_ \_ \_    \_ \_ \_

N V T U    Q V U    P G G


E Z K R D G N N C    Z M C    R O D Z J

\_ \_ \_ \_ \_ \_ \_ \_ \_    \_ \_ \_    \_ \_ \_ \_ \_

G B M T F I P P E    B O E    T Q F B L


S Q T S G E T K K X    S N    G H R

\_ \_ \_ \_ \_ \_ \_ \_ \_ \_    \_ \_    \_ \_ \_

U S V U I G V M N Z    U P    I J T


M D H F G A N Q    E N Q    Z K K    Z Q D

\_ \_ \_ \_ \_ \_ \_ \_    \_ \_ \_    \_ \_ \_    \_ \_ \_

O F J H I C P S    G P S    B M M    B S F


L D L A D Q R    N E    N M D    A N C X

\_ \_ \_ \_ \_ \_ \_    \_ \_    \_ \_ \_    \_ \_ \_ \_

N F N C F S T    P G    P O F    C P E Z

## Fruits of the Spirit

The big screen, television, and magazines bombard us with images of how we should strive to look and what we should materialistically obtain. These materialist goals set us up for disappointment and dissatisfaction with our lives when we can't keep up pretences in comparison to someone else's life.  We don't have to dress in rags or drive vehicles that break down every two feet, but watch your motivations for acquiring possessions. Instead of comparing ourselves and our belongings to others, we should view ourselves through the eyes of God.  In Psalm 139:14 it says, "I praise you because I am fearfully and wonderfully made."

God has created you as he intended.  He has created you in his own image. Focus on your internal attributes instead of your outward appearance and possessions. Strive to be Christ-like, a person of virtue. According to Webster's New World College Dictionary fourth edition, virtue is general moral excellence; right action and thinking; goodness or morality. Your value is found in the God that created you and the Savior that redeemed you, strive for your inner beauty.

From the book of Galatians, list "The fruits of the Spirit."

1.                                6.


2.                                7.


3.                                8.


4.                                9.


5.

**Fruits of the Spirit Puzzles:**

Whatever
Virtues
Goodness
Your Words and Actions in the Name of Jesus

**Whatever!**

Directions:  Fit the words in bold print, from the Bible verse, onto the corresponding lines below.

```
_ _ _ _ _ _W_ _ _ _ _

      _ _ _H_

_ _ _ _ _ _ _ _A_ _ _: _

         T_ _ _

      _ _ _ _E

        _ _V_ _ _

        E_ _ _ _ _ _ _ _

          _ _R_
```

Finally, brothers, whatever is **true**, whatever is **noble**, whatever is **right**, whatever is **pure**, whatever is **lovely**, whatever is **admirable** if anything is **excellent** or **praiseworthy** think about such things.  Philippians 4:8

24

**Virtues**

Step 1:  Circle the word in the groups of four below that does not belong with the other words. Fit the circled words into the bible verse below.

Step 2:  One letter of the circled words per space.

Step 3:  a few words have the same number of letters in them, so I gave you the first letter of some of the words to narrow down your choice.

| | | | | |
|---|---|---|---|---|
| Pigtails | loved | hotdog | humility | leaves |
| Kindness | pink | hamburger | towel | grass |
| Ponytails | yellow | pizza | washcloth | chosen |
| Braids | blue | gentleness | soap | sticks |

| | | | | |
|---|---|---|---|---|
| Yard light | compass | candy bar | rose | car |
| Flashlight | atlas | holy | love | truck |
| Streetlight | compassion | gum | petunias | unity |
| Patience | globe | sucker | daffodils | van |

Therefore as God's __ __ __ __ __ __ people, h __ __ __

and dearly __ __ __ __ __, clothe yourselves with

__ __ __ __ __ __ __ __ __ __ __, k __ __ __ __ __ __ __,

__ __ __ __ __ __ __ __, g __ __ __ __ __ __ __ __ __ __ and

__ __ __ __ __ __ __ __. And over all these virtues put on

__ __ __ __, which binds them all together in perfect

u __ __ __ __.

## Goodness

Directions: Place the letter on the lines that corresponds with the number to finish the direction from God's word.

1. p
2. s
3. e
4. m
5. z
6. d
7. v
8. i
9. x          Therefore as we have opportunity...
10. a
11. l
12. y
13. r   $\overline{11}$ $\overline{3}$ $\overline{16}$   $\overline{21}$ $\overline{2}$   $\overline{6}$ $\overline{15}$   $\overline{26}$ $\overline{15}$ $\overline{15}$ $\overline{6}$
14. f
15. o   $\overline{16}$ $\overline{15}$   $\overline{10}$ $\overline{11}$ $\overline{11}$   $\overline{1}$ $\overline{3}$ $\overline{15}$ $\overline{1}$ $\overline{11}$ $\overline{3}$
16. t
17. b
18. k
19. w   $\overline{3}$ $\overline{2}$ $\overline{1}$ $\overline{3}$ $\overline{23}$ $\overline{8}$ $\overline{10}$ $\overline{11}$ $\overline{11}$ $\overline{12}$   $\overline{16}$ $\overline{20}$ $\overline{15}$ $\overline{2}$ $\overline{3}$
20. h
21. u   $\overline{\phantom{0}}$ $\overline{\phantom{0}}$ $\overline{\phantom{0}}$   $\overline{\phantom{0}}$ $\overline{\phantom{0}}$ $\overline{\phantom{0}}$ $\overline{\phantom{0}}$ $\overline{\phantom{0}}$ $\overline{\phantom{0}}$
22. q
23. c   19 20 15    17 3 11 15 25 26
24. j
25. n
26. g

$\overline{16}$ $\overline{15}$   $\overline{16}$ $\overline{20}$ $\overline{3}$   $\overline{14}$ $\overline{10}$ $\overline{4}$ $\overline{8}$ $\overline{11}$ $\overline{12}$   $\overline{15}$ $\overline{14}$

$\overline{17}$ $\overline{3}$ $\overline{11}$ $\overline{8}$ $\overline{7}$ $\overline{3}$ $\overline{13}$ $\overline{2}$.   $\overline{26}$ $\overline{10}$ $\overline{11}$. 6:10

## Your Words and Actions
## In The Name of Jesus

Intersect the number and the bold letter to find the letter to place on the corresponding lines below, and solve the puzzle.

|   | A | B | C | D | E |
|---|---|---|---|---|---|
| **1** | R | L | E | 9 | T |
| **2** | F | H | G | A | B |
| **3** | C | M | 1 | K | U |
| **4** | N | J | W | Q | S |
| **5** | Y | X | D | I | V |
| **6** | P | 7 | Z | 2 | O |

2D 4A 5C    4C 2B 2D 1E 1C 5E 1C 1A    5A 6E 3E    5C 6E

4C 2B 1C 1E 2B 1C 1A    5D 4A    4C 6E 1A 5C    6E 1A

5C 1C 1C 5C,    5C 6E    5D 1E    2D 1B 1B    5D 4A    1E 2B 1C

4A 2D 3B 1C    6E 2A    1E 2B 1C    1B 6E 1A 5C

4B 1C 4E 3E 4E,    2C 5D 5E 5D 4A 2C    1E 2B 2D 4A 3D 4E

1E 6E    2C 6E 5C    1E 2B 1C    2A 2D 1E 2B 1C 1A

1E 2B 1A 6E 3E 2C 2B    2B 5D 3B.

## God's Promises

Throughout our life we have all experienced difficult trials such as the loss of a friendship or the loss of a loved one.  But remember, as we concentrate on the problems of today, God has the bigger picture of our lives and salvation in mind. Isaiah 55:8 tells us, "For my thoughts are not your thoughts, neither are your ways my ways," declares the Lord.  His plans are not our plans but I believe that even the little things that annoy us on a daily basis, happen for a purpose. In the big problems, and the little annoyances of life, rest in the assurance of God's promises.

Look up Psalm 145:13 and record the second half of the verse here "...
The

_____

_____."

Some days, it seems we run from one problem to another. It might be those simple annoyances or it could be something harder to accept or deal with. Perhaps the irritation of misplacing your car keys kept you minutes away from an accident. Remember we can't see the big picture God has planned. In your impatience and frustration let God's words strengthen you.

In Joshua and 1 Kings God's promises are described as never failing. In Acts and Galatians it states, God's promises are fulfilled on schedule. God promises Christ's intercession on our behalf, victorious living and eternal life. In your day to day walk through this life, trust in the promises God has given you.

**God's Promises Puzzles:**

Assurance
Problems, Problems
Protection
Promise for the Future

**Assurance**

ABCDEFGHIJKLMNOPQRSTUVWXYZ

On the lines below write the letter that comes between the top and bottom letter to finish the verse.

**And we know,**

S G Z S    H M    Z K K    S G H M F R    F N C    V N Q J R

_ _ _ _    _ _    _ _ _    _ _ _ _ _ _    _ _ _    _ _ _ _ _

U I B U    J O    B M M    U I J O H T    H P E    X P S L T


E N Q    S G D    F N N C    N E    S G N R D    V G N

_ _ _    _ _ _    _ _ _ _    _ _    _ _ _ _ _    _ _ _

G P S    U I F    H P P E    P G    U I P T F    X I P


K N U D    G H L    V G N    G Z U D    A D D M

_ _ _ _    _ _ _    _ _ _    _ _ _ _    _ _ _ _

M P W F    I J N    X I P    I B W F    C F F O


B Z K K D C    Z B B N Q    C H M F

_ _ _ _ _ _    _ _ _ _ _    _ _ _ _

D B M M F E    B D D P S    E J O H


S N    G H R    O T Q O N R D

_ _    _ _ _    _ _ _ _ _ _ _

U P    I J T    Q V S Q P T F

## Problems, Problems

Intersect the number and the bold letter to find the letter to place on the corresponding lines below, and solve the puzzle.

|     | **A** | **B** | **C** | **D** | **E** |
|-----|-------|-------|-------|-------|-------|
| **1** | R | L | E | P | T |
| **2** | F | H | G | A | B |
| **3** | C | M | Z | K | U |
| **4** | N | J | 4 | 6 | S |
| **5** | Y | O | D | I | V |

$\overline{2C}$ $\overline{5B}$ $\overline{5C}$  $\overline{5D}$ $\overline{4E}$  $\overline{5B}$ $\overline{3E}$ $\overline{1A}$  $\overline{1A}$ $\overline{1C}$ $\overline{2A}$ $\overline{3E}$  $\overline{2C}$ $\overline{1C}$  $\overline{2D}$ $\overline{4A}$ $\overline{5C}$

$\overline{4E}$ $\overline{1E}$ $\overline{1A}$ $\overline{1C}$ $\overline{4A}$ $\overline{2C}$ $\overline{1E}$ $\overline{2B}$  $\overline{2D}$ $\overline{4A}$  $\overline{1C}$ $\overline{5E}$ $\overline{1C}$ $\overline{1A}$ -

$\overline{1D}$ $\overline{1R}$  $\overline{1C}$ $\overline{4E}$ $\overline{1C}$ $\overline{4A}$ $\overline{1E}$  $\overline{2B}$ $\overline{1C}$ $\overline{1B}$ $\overline{1D}$  $\overline{5D}$ $\overline{4A}$  $\overline{1E}$ $\overline{5D}$ $\overline{3B}$ $\overline{1C}$

$\overline{5B}$ $\overline{2A}$  $\overline{1E}$ $\overline{1A}$ $\overline{5B}$ $\overline{3E}$ $\overline{2E}$ $\overline{1B}$ $\overline{1C}$

$\overline{1D}$ $\overline{4E}$ $\overline{2D}$ $\overline{1B}$ $\overline{3B}$  $\overline{4C}$ : $\overline{4D}$

## Protection

1. p
2. s
3. e
4. m
5. z
6. t
7. v
8. a
9. x
10. i
11. l
12. y
13. r
14. f
15. o
16. d
17. b
18. k
19. w
20. h
21. u
22. q
23. c
24. j
25. n
26. g

$\overline{17}\ \overline{21}\ \overline{6}\quad \overline{6}\ \overline{20}\ \overline{3}\quad \overline{11}\ \overline{15}\ \overline{13}\ \overline{16}\quad \overline{10}\ \overline{2}$

$\overline{14}\ \overline{8}\ \overline{10}\ \overline{6}\ \overline{20}\ \overline{14}\ \overline{21}\ \overline{11}\quad \overline{8}\ \overline{25}\ \overline{16}\quad \overline{20}\ \overline{3}$

$\overline{19}\ \overline{10}\ \overline{11}\ \overline{11}\quad \overline{2}\ \overline{6}\ \overline{13}\ \overline{3}\ \overline{25}\ \overline{26}\ \overline{6}\ \overline{20}\ \overline{3}\ \overline{25}$

$\overline{8}\ \overline{25}\ \overline{16}\quad \overline{1}\ \overline{13}\ \overline{15}\ \overline{6}\ \overline{3}\ \overline{23}\ \overline{6}\quad \overline{12}\ \overline{15}\ \overline{21}$

$\overline{14}\ \overline{13}\ \overline{15}\ \overline{4}\quad \overline{6}\ \overline{20}\ \overline{3}\quad \overline{3}\ \overline{7}\ \overline{10}\ \overline{11}\quad \overline{15}\ \overline{25}\ \overline{3}.$

2 $\overline{6}\ \overline{20}\ \overline{3}\ \overline{2}\ \overline{2}\ \overline{8}\ \overline{11}\ \overline{15}\ \overline{25}\ \overline{10}\ \overline{8}\ \overline{25}\ \overline{2}$3:3

## Promise for a Future

Intersect the number and the bold letter to find the letter to place on the corresponding lines below, and solve the puzzle.

|   | A | B | C | D | E |
|---|---|---|---|---|---|
| **1** | R | L | E | 9 | T |
| **2** | F | H | G | A | B |
| **3** | C | M | Z | K | U |
| **4** | N | J | W | Q | S |
| **5** | Y | X | D | I | V |
| **6** | P | 7 | O | 3 | 4 |

2A 6C 1A 5D   3D 4A 6C 4C   1E 2B 1C   6A 1B 2D 4A 4E   5D

2B 2D 5E 1C   2A 6C 1A   5A 6C 3E   5C 1C 3A 1B 2D 1A 1C 4E

1E 2B 1C   1B 6C 1A 5C   6A 1B 2D 4A 4E   1E 6C

6A 1A 6C 4E 6A 1C 1A   5A 6C 3E   2D 4A 5C   4A 6C 1E

1E 6C   2B 2D 1A 3B   5A 6C 3E   6A 1B 2D 4A 4E

1E 6C   2C 5D 5E 1C   5A 6C 3E   2B 6C 6A 1C

2D 4A 5C   2D   2A 3E 1E 3E 1A 1C

## Forgiveness

In the book of Isaiah and in Webster's New World College Dictionary, forgiveness is described as an act of pardon.

"For if you forgive men when they sin against you, your heavenly Father will also forgive you. But if you do not forgive men their sins, your Father will not forgive your sins." Matthew 6:14-15

This verse from Matthew is not a suggestion. It is cause and effect. If you forgive, then your Father in heaven will forgive you. When you hold onto past hurts, the person you believed wronged you may not even realize your anger or resentment. The negativity only festers in your soul. It consumes time and energy as you focus on the injustice you have received. Even if you have been wronged, you are usually the only person suffering.

God gives us a specific guideline to help us overcome hurts or trespasses someone has done to us. In James 5:16 it says, "Therefore confess your sins to each other and pray for each other so that you may be healed."

What? Pray for someone that has insulted, harmed, or angered me? James 5:16 continues, "The prayer of a righteous man is powerful and effective." Prayer is powerful and effective. It can heal you. But the verse states, prayer of a righteous man. Resentful and bitter is not righteous. Pray for yourself to be understanding and forgiving as God forgave you in Christ. Pray for the person that has trespassed against you and perhaps you will be able to understand them better.

Forgiveness frees us from resentment and bitterness to lead a joyful life. You don't have to carry the burden of another person's actions. Granting forgiveness lifts the darkness. Through grace, which means undeserved favor, we can let it go as God has let our transgressions go as we ask forgiveness. Through Christ's selflessness, forgiveness is possible.

**Forgiveness Puzzles:**

Sunset
Show Compassion
Turn the Other Cheek
Forgiveness

## Sunset

| In | Your | Purple | Four | Anger |
|---|---|---|---|---|
| Pink | Do | Three | Not | Sin |
| Do | Green | Not | Let | Five |
| Six | The | Sun | Go | Black |
| Down | While | Four | You | Two |
| Black | Are | Violet | Still | Angry |
| Yellow | Green | And | Do | Not |
| Give | The | Red | Pink | Orange |
| Blue | Devil | A | Two | Foothold |

Direction#1:  Circle all the number words and add the amounts together.  Place that number on the blank below next to the word Ephesians, and then cross out the number words.

Direction #2:   Cross out all the color words.

Direction #3:  Place the remaining words in the order they appear from left to right on the blanks below.

_____ _____ _____ _____ _____ _____ _____ _____ _____

_____ _____ _____ _____ _____ _____ _____ _____

_____ _____ ____ ____ ____ _____ _____ ____

_____. Ephesians 4: ___- 27

## Show Compassion

ABCDEFGHIJKLMNOPQRSTUVWXYZ

On the lines below write the letter that comes between the top and bottom letter to finish the verse.

```
A  D     J  H  M  C     Z  M  C
B  E     K  I  N  D     A  N  D
C  F     L  J  O  E     B  O  E
```

```
B  N  L  O  Z  R  R  H  N  M  Z  S  D     S  N     N  M  D
C  O  M  P  A  S  S  I  O  N  A  T  E     T  O     O  N  E
D  P  N  Q  B  T  T  J  P  O  B  U  F     U  P     P  O  F
```

```
Z  M  N  S  G  D  Q     E  N  Q  F  H  U  H  M  F
A  N  O  T  H  E  R     F  O  R  G  I  V  I  N  G
B  O  P  U  I  F  S     G  P  S  H  J  W  J  O  H
```

```
Z  R  F  N  C     E  N  Q  F  Z  U  D     X  N  T
A  S  G  O  D     F  O  R  G  A  V  E     Y  O  U.
B  T  H  P  E     G  P  S  H  B  W  F     Z  P  V
```

```
A  Z  R  D  C     N  M     D  O  G  D  R  H  Z  M  R
B  A  S  E  D     O  N     E  P  H  E  S  I  A  N  S   4:32
C  B  T  F  E     P  O     F  Q  I  F  T  J  B  O  T
```

## Turn the Other Cheek

Intersect the number and the bold letter to find the letter to place on the corresponding lines below, and solve the puzzle.

|   | **A** | **B** | **C** | **D** | **E** |
|---|---|---|---|---|---|
| **1** | R | L | E | 9 | T |
| **2** | F | H | G | A | B |
| **3** | C | M | Z | K | U |
| **4** | N | J | W | Q | S |
| **5** | Y | X | D | I | V |
| **6** | P | 4 | O | 2 | 3 |

__ __   __ __ __   __ __ __ __ __   __ __ __ __
5C 6C   4A 6C 1E   1A 1C 6A 2D 5A   1C 5E 5D 1B

__ __ __ __   __ __ __ __   __ __   __ __ __ __ __ __
4C 5D 1E 2B   1C 5E 5D 1B   6C 1A   5D 4A 4E 3E 1B 1E

__ __ __ __   __ __ __ __ __ __,   __ __ __   __ __ __ __
4C 5D 1E 2B   5D 4A 4E 3E 1B 1E   2E 3E 1E   4C 5D 1E 2B

__ __ __ __ __ __ __ __,   __ __ __ __ __ __ __
2E 1B 1C 4E 4E 5D 4A 2C   2E 1C 3A 2D 3E 4E 1C

__ __   __ __ __ __   __ __ __   __ __ __ __
6C 2A   1E 2B 5D 4E   5A 6C 3E   4C 1C 1A 1C

__ __ __ __ __ __   __ __   __ __ __ __   __ __ __   __ __ __
3A 2D 1B 1B 1C 5C   4E 6C   1E 2B 2D 1E   5A 6C 3E   3B 2D 5A

__ __ __ __ __ __ __   __   __ __ __ __ __ __ __ __.
5D 4A 2B 1C 1A 5D 1E   2D   2E 1B 1C 4E 4E 5D 4A 2C

1 Peter __: __
             6E  1D

## Forgiveness

In the pairs of letters below, find the message from God on how to act with our daily frustrations.  Starting at **BD**, circle the first letter of the select pair The second letter of the pair will tell you which direction to move.  L for left, R for right, U for up, and D for down.  Place circled letters in order on the lines below as you go.

| **BD** | FR | TU | ER | RR | AD | CD | AD | HU | JD |
|--------|----|----|----|----|----|----|----|----|----|
| ER | AD | SL | HU | TL | ND | TR | YR | VR | ED |
| JU | RD | ER | HR | OU | DR | FD | GR | IU | WD |
| ID | WL | AR | CU | NL | JR | OR | RU | AD | HL |
| TR | HR | EU | TL | EU | GD | RL | EL | TD | EL |
| PR | ED | AR | PR | ID | RL | ND | VU | EL | YD |
| SD | EL | AD | VL | EL | NR | SD | NR | ED | BD |
| YD | CU | NL | GR | AR | IU | TR | OU | AR | ND |
| OD | LL | RR | AU | EL | OL | XD | WD | TD | OL |
| UR | MD | ID | AR | VU | YU | RD | OL | HR | ED |
| CR | AR | YR | HU | IU | HU | TL | OU | DL | R |

B __ __ __   __ __ __ __   __ __ __   __ __ __ __

__ __ __   __ __ __ __ __ __   __ __ __ __ __ __ __

__ __ __ __ __ __ __ __   __ __ __   __ __ __

__ __ __ __   __ __ __ __ __ __ __   __ __ __

__ __ __ __ __   __ R.

## In Conclusion

Some people believe that there are no directions that came with this life journey, but that isn't true. God has given us guidelines through His word, the Holy Bible. Directions, that if we follow them, will make our own lives better. 2 Timothy 3:16-17 states, "All Scripture is God-breathed and is useful for teaching, rebuking, correcting and training in righteousness, so that the man of God may be thoroughly equipped for every good work."

Even the United States of America was founded by men that believed in One True God and principles and commandments found in His Holy Word. Our fourth president, James Madison said, "We've staked our future on our ability to follow the Ten Commandments with all our heart. We have staked the whole future of American civilization, not upon the power of government, far from it. We've staked the future of all our political institutions upon our capacity… to sustain ourselves according to the Ten Commandments of God." (1778 to the General Assembly of the State of Virginia)

You are responsible for your own actions so, "Whatever happens, conduct yourselves in a manner worthy of the gospel of Christ." Philippians 1:29

The guidelines have been laid out for you. Encourage one another in your journey through this world as you prepare for eternal live with Christ.

**In Conclusion Puzzles:**

Relax
Guidelines
Prepare for the Devil's Schemes
Filled with Hope

**Relax**

A Skills Puzzle. Solve the math problem and match the letter to the number below.

$9÷3=$ __   $63-59=$ __   $5x4-11=$ __   $12x2=$ __   $20-5=$ __   $5x5-20=$ __   $16-6=$ __
    N          A          R          W       F          D          H

$30÷2-1=$ __   $200-198=$ __   $5+7-5=$ __   $35x2-47=$ __   $64÷8=$ __   $60÷2-5=$ __
    I          T          G          Y          C          M

$3x3-8=$ __   $11x1=$ __   $3x7=$ __   $51-33=$ __   $12÷2=$ __   $51÷3=$ __
    O          L          S          B          E          U

$3x7-8=$ __   $20÷2+12=$ __   $2x5+2=$ __   $64÷2-16=$ __   $2x9+1$ __
    V          K          P          X          Q

__ __   __ __ __   __ __   __ __ __ __ __ __ __
5  1    3  1  2    18  6    4  3  16  14  1  17  21

__ __ __ __ __   __ __ __ __ __ __ __ __,
4  18  1  17  2    4  3  23  2  10  14  3  7

__ __ __   __ __   __ __ __ __ __ __ __ __ __,
18  17  2    14  3    6  13  6  9  23  2  10  14  3  7

__ __   __ __ __ __ __ __   __ __ __
18  23    12  9  4  23  6  9    4  3  5

__ __ __ __ __ __ __ __,   __ __ __ __
12  6  2  14  2  14  1  3    24  14  2  10

__ __ __ __ __ __ __ __ __ __ __ __,   __ __ __ __ __ __ __
2  10  4  3  22  21  7  14  13  14  3  7    12  9  6  21  6  3  2

__ __ __ __   __ __ __ __ __ __ __ __   __ __   __ __ __.
23  1  17  9    9  6  19  17  6  21  2  21    2  1    7  1  5

## Guidelines

1. p
2. s
3. e
4. m
5. z
6. d
7. v
8. i
9. x
10. a
11. l
12. y
13. r
14. f
15. o
16. t
17. b
18. k
19. w
20. h
21. u
22. q
23. c
24. j
25. n
26. g

$$\overline{17}\ \overline{3}\quad \overline{24}\ \overline{15}\ \overline{12}\ \overline{14}\ \overline{21}\ \overline{11}\quad \overline{10}\ \overline{11}\ \overline{19}\ \overline{10}\ \overline{12}\ \overline{2},$$

$$\overline{1}\ \overline{13}\ \overline{10}\ \overline{12}\quad \overline{23}\ \overline{15}\ \overline{25}\ \overline{16}\ \overline{8}\ \overline{25}\ \overline{21}\ \overline{10}\ \overline{11}\ \overline{11}\ \overline{12},$$

$$\overline{26}\ \overline{8}\ \overline{7}\ \overline{3}\quad \overline{16}\ \overline{20}\ \overline{10}\ \overline{25}\ \overline{18}\ \overline{2}\quad \overline{8}\ \overline{25}\quad \overline{10}\ \overline{11}\ \overline{11}$$

$$\overline{23}\ \overline{8}\ \overline{13}\ \overline{23}\quad \overline{21}\ \overline{4}\quad \overline{2}\quad \overline{16}\ \overline{10}\ \overline{25}\ \overline{23}\ \overline{3}\ \overline{2},\quad \overline{14}\ \overline{15}\ \overline{13}$$

$$\overline{16}\ \overline{20}\ \overline{8}\ \overline{2}\quad \overline{8}\ \overline{2}\quad \overline{26}\ \overline{15}\ \overline{6}\ \overline{2}\quad \overline{19}\ \overline{8}\ \overline{11}\ \overline{11}$$

$$\overline{14}\ \overline{15}\ \overline{13}\quad \overline{12}\ \overline{15}\ \overline{21}\quad \overline{8}\ \overline{25}\quad \overline{23}\ \overline{20}\ \overline{13}\ \overline{8}\ \overline{2}\ \overline{16}$$

$$\overline{24}\ \overline{3}\ \overline{2}\ \overline{21}\ \overline{2}.$$

## Prepare for the Devil's Schemes

Solve the math problem and match the letter to the number below.

3+3= __     63-61= __     5x4-13= __     42÷2= __     19-5= __     15÷3= __     16-5= __
   N          A          R       W      F       D       H

30÷2-11= __     200-199= __     5+7-4= __     35x2-60= __     36÷2= __     60÷2-6= __
    I          T        G       Y      C       M

4x3-9= __     11x2= __     3x3= __     50-34= __     100-32÷4= __     9x3= __
   O        L       S       B        E      U

36-21= __     20÷2+2= __     2x5+3= __
   V        K       P

Finally,   __ __   __ __ __ __ __ __   __ __   __ __ __
          16 17   9  1  7  3  6  8   4  6   1 11 17

__ __ __ __   __ __ __   __ __   __ __ __
22  3  7  5   2  6  5   4  6   11  4  9

__ __ __ __ __ __   __ __ __ __ __   __ __ __
24  4  8  11  1 10   13  3 21 17  7   13 27  1

__ __   __ __ __   __ __ __ __   __ __ __ __ __   __ __
3  6   1 11 17   14 27 22 22   2  7 24  3  7   3 14

__ __ __   __ __   __ __ __ __   __ __ __   __ __ __
8  3  5   9  3   1 11  2  1   10  3 27   18  2  6

__ __ __ __   __ __ __ __ __   __ __ __ __ __ __
1  2 12 17   9  1  2  6  5   2  8  2  4  6  9  1

__ __ __   __ __ __ __ __ __   __ __ __ __ __ __ __
1 11 17   5 17 15  4 22  9   9 18 11 17 24 17  9

Even Jesus was tempted by the devil. Remember to call on the Lord and he will provide a way to stand up under temptation and help you walk away.

"No temptation has seized you except what is common to man. And God is faithful; he will not let you be tempted beyond what you can bear. But when you are tempted, he will also provide a way out so that you can stand up under it." 1 Corinthians 10:13

### Filled with Hope

Let God's words strengthen you. Intersect the number and the bold letter to find the letter to place on the corresponding lines below, and solve the puzzle.

|   | **A** | **B** | **C** | **D** | **E** |
|---|---|---|---|---|---|
| **1** | R | L | E | P | T |
| **2** | F | H | G | A | B |
| **3** | C | M | Z | K | U |
| **4** | N | J | 4 | W | S |
| **5** | Y | O | D | I | V |

3B 2D 5A   1E 2B 1C   2C 5B 5C   5B 2A   2B 5B 1D 1C

2A 5D 1B 1B   5A 5B 3E   4D 5D 1E 2B   2D 1B 1B   4B 5B 5A

2D 4A 5C   1D 1C 2D 3A 1C   2D 4E   5A 5B 3E   1E 1A 3E 4E 1E

5D 4A   2B 5D 3B, 4E 5B   5A 5B 3E   3B 2D 5A

5B 5E 1C 1A 2A 1B 5B 4D   4D 5D 1E 2B   2B 5B 1D 1C   2E 5A

1E 2B 1C   1D 5B 4D 1C 1A   5B 2A   1E 2B 1C   2B 5B 1B 5A

4E 1D 5D 1A 5D 1E.

46

## Puzzle Answer Key

### Daily Frustrations Page 11
Philippians 1:27

Answer Key:

Whatever happens conduct yourselves in a manner worthy of the gospel of Christ.

~ * ~

### Good Verses Evil Page 12

Answer Key:

Love must be sincere; hate what is evil, cling to what is good.
Romans 12:9

~ * ~

### Lean on Me Page 13
Galatians 6:2

Answer Key:

2x8= $\underline{16}$   5x4-3= $\underline{17}$   40÷10= $\underline{4}$   6+6= $\underline{12}$   22÷2= $\underline{11}$
$\quad$ U $\qquad\quad$ A $\qquad\quad$ O $\qquad\quad$ D $\qquad\quad$ R

8x2÷8= $\underline{2}$   30÷2-10= $\underline{5}$   4003-4002= $\underline{1}$   5+7-4= $\underline{8}$
$\quad\quad$ H $\qquad\qquad$ I $\qquad\qquad\quad$ W $\qquad\quad\quad$ B

999-993= $\underline{6}$   27÷3= $\underline{9}$   2x5+3= $\underline{13}$   64÷4-1= $\underline{15}$
$\qquad\quad$ F $\qquad\quad$ S $\qquad\qquad$ E $\qquad\qquad\quad$ N

15÷5= $\underline{3}$   100÷10= $\underline{10}$   46÷2-9= $\underline{14}$   10÷2+2= $\underline{7}$
$\qquad$ L $\qquad\qquad$ T $\qquad\qquad$ C $\qquad\qquad$ Y

Carry each others burdens, and in this way, you will fulfill the law of Christ.

~ * ~

## Bite Your Tongue Page 14
2 Timothy 2:24

Answer Key:

The Lord's servant must not quarrel, instead, he must be kind to everyone, able to teach, not resentful.

~ * ~

## New in Christ Page 18
Colossians 3:8

Answer Key:

But now you must

rid yourselves of all such things as these: anger, rage, malice, slander, and filthy language from your lips.

~ * ~

## Hush Page 19

Answer Key:

Do not let any unwholesome talk come out of your mouths but only what is helpful for building others up according to their needs.   Ephesians 4:29

~ * ~

## Self-Control Page 20
James 1:19-21

Answer Key:

Everyone should be...

quick to listen, slow to speak and slow to become angry and humbly accept the word planted in you which can save you.

~ * ~

## Speak Truthfully Page 21
Ephesians 4:25

Answer Key:

Therefore each of you must put off falsehood and speak truthfully to his neighbor for all are members of one body.

~ * ~

## Whatever Page 24
Based on Philippians 4:8

Answer Key:

Praiseworthy
Right
Admirable
True
Noble
Lovely
Excellent
Pure

~ * ~

## Virtues Page 25
Colossians 3:12 & 14

Answer Key:

Therefore as God's chosen people, holy and dearly loved, clothe yourselves with compassion, kindness, humility, gentleness and patience.

And over all these virtues put on love, which binds them all together in perfect unity.

~ * ~

## Goodness Page 26

Answer Key:

Let us do good to all people especially those who belong to the family of believers. Galatians 6:10

~ * ~

## Your Words and Actions In The Name of Jesus Page 27

Answer Key:

And whatever you do, whether in word or deed, do it all in the name of the Lord Jesus, giving thanks to God the Father through him.     Colossians 3:17

~ * ~

## Assurance Page 30
### Romans 8:28

Answer Key:

And we know,

That in all things God works for the good of those who love Him who have been called according to his purpose.

~ * ~

## Problems, Problems Page 31

Answer Key:

God is our refuge and strength, an ever-present help in time of trouble. Psalm 46

~ * ~

## Protection Page 32

Answer Key:

But the Lord is faithful and he will strengthen and protect you from the evil one. 2 Thessalonians 3:3

~ * ~

## Promise for a Future Page 33
Jeremiah 29:11

Answer Key:

For I know the plans I have for you declares the Lord plans to prosper you and not to harm you plans to give you hope and a future.

~ * ~

## Sunset Page 36

Answer Key:

In your anger do not sin. Do not let the sun go down while you are still angry, and do not give the devil a foothold.
Ephesians 4:26-27

~ * ~

## Show Compassion Page 37

Answer Key:

"Be kind and compassionate to one another forgiving as God forgave you." Based on Ephesians 4:32

~ * ~

## Turn the Other Cheek Page 38

Answer Key:

Do not repay evil with evil or insult with insult, but with blessing, because of this you were called so that you may inherit a blessing.
1 Peter 3:9

~ * ~

## Forgiveness Page 39
### Colossians 3:13

Answer Key:

Bear with each other and forgive whatever grievances you may have against one another.

~ * ~

## Relax Page 42
### Philippians 4:6

Answer Key:

9÷3= <u>3</u>   63-59= <u>4</u>   5x4-11= <u>9</u>   12x2= <u>24</u>   20-5= <u>15</u>   5x5-20= <u>5</u>   16-6= <u>10</u>
N          A          R          W          F          D          H

30÷2-1= <u>14</u>   200-198= <u>2</u>   5+7-5= <u>7</u>   35x2-47= <u>23</u>   64÷8= <u>8</u>   60÷2-5= <u>25</u>
I          T          G          Y          C          M

3x3-8= <u>1</u>   11x1= <u>11</u>   3x7= <u>21</u>   51-33= <u>18</u>   12÷2= <u>6</u>   51÷3= <u>17</u>
O          L          S          B          E          U

3x7-8= <u>13</u>   20÷2+12= <u>22</u>   2x5+2= <u>12</u>   64÷2-16= <u>16</u>   2x9+1= <u>19</u>
V          K          P          X          Q

Do not be anxious about anything, but in everything, by prayer and petition, with thanksgiving, present your requests to God.

~ * ~

## Guidelines Page 43
### 1Thessalonians 5:16-18

Answer Key:

Be joyful always, pray continually, give thanks in all circumstances, for this is God's will for you in Christ Jesus.

~ * ~

## Prepare for the Devil's Schemes Page 44
Ephesians 6:10-11

Answer Key:

3+3= $\underline{6}$    63-61= $\underline{2}$    5x4-13= $\underline{7}$    42÷2= $\underline{21}$    19-5= $\underline{14}$    15÷3= $\underline{5}$    16-5= $\underline{11}$
  N              A                R                  W                F              D              H

30÷2-11= $\underline{4}$    200-199= $\underline{1}$    5+7-4= $\underline{8}$    35x2-60= $\underline{10}$    36÷2= $\underline{18}$    60÷2-6= $\underline{24}$
      I                  T                G                  Y                  C                M

4x3-9= $\underline{3}$    11x2= $\underline{22}$    3x3= $\underline{9}$    50-34= $\underline{23}$    100-32÷4= $\underline{17}$    9x3= $\underline{27}$
    O              L              S              B                  E                  U

36-21= $\underline{15}$    20÷2+2= $\underline{12}$    2x5+3= $\underline{13}$
      V                K                P

Be strong in the Lord and in his mighty power. Put on the full armor of God so that you can take stand against the devil's schemes.

~ * ~

## Filled with Hope Page 46
Romans 15:13

Answer Key:

May the God of hope fill you with all joy and peace as you trust in him, so you may overflow with hope by the power of the Holy Spirit.

**~ END ~**

www.ingramcontent.com/pod-product-compliance
Lightning Source LLC
Chambersburg PA
CBHW042055040426
42447CB00003B/238